Elvis Presley 1956

Elvis Presley 1956

Photographs by Marvin Israel

Edited and Designed by Martin Harrison

Harry N. Abrams, Inc., Publishers

Marvin Israel

Marvin Israel was one of those rare mavericks whose creativity flowed at the intersections of different disciplines, including painting, the graphic arts, photography, art direction, and design. He first took up photography in 1953, while studying graphic design under the legendary art director Alexey Brodovitch. Had he lived to see this, his first book, one hopes he would have been delighted; he would probably have been surprised. For his photography was largely confined to a six-year period in the 1950s and is, compared to his widely influential contribution as an art director, virtually unknown today. Yet the surviving archive of his photographs is abundant proof that Marvin, if less prolific than the full-time professionals, deserves a prominent place in what has become known as the New York School of photography. Allied to his innate feeling for graphic structure, his photographs unfailingly share the New York School's values of spontaneity, movement, and a raw realism. He was committed to exploring the cumulative effect of images-in-series, and his photographs of Elvis amply demonstrate his attachment to the pace and immediacy of the filmic sequence.

Marvin was born in Syracuse, New York, in 1924. Disinclined to join his family's clothing business, his only ambition was to become an artist. Shortly after his marriage to the talented artist Margaret Ponce in 1950, the couple moved to Paris, where the Galerie Arnaud staged the first one-man exhibition of Marvin's paintings in 1952. Back in the U.S.A. the following year he enrolled at Yale University to study under

Josef Albers, but switched to a course run by Brodovitch and graduated with an M.F.A. in graphic design. Unable to subsist solely on sales of his paintings, he took a job in the art department of *Seventeen* magazine. On becoming art director in 1955 he was responsible for commissioning many distinguished photographers, including Diane and Allan Arbus, Robert Frank, and Lee Friedlander. But Marvin reserved two plum *Seventeen* photographic assignments for himself: he recorded James Dean on the set of *Giant* in 1955 and Elvis Presley in 1956. In the context of a mainstream publication aimed at teenage girls, Israel's stark, uncompromising black and whites must have appeared unsettling, and only two of his five-hundred photographs of Elvis were published at the time.

Art director of Atlantic Records for several years and of *Harper's Bazaar* from 1961 to 1963, Israel was also renowned for his collaborations, on books and exhibitions, with Diane Arbus and Richard Avedon. In the 1970s, as well as being an influential teacher and catalyst for the talents of others, he found his own style as a painter and achieved some recognition for his powerful draftsmanship and originality. He died of a heart attack in Dallas, Texas, in the spring of 1984, while working on Avedon's "In the American West" project. Until now his compelling photo-documents of Elvis, taken in the last few months before informal access to the star was vetoed by his management, have remained unpublished and unknown. They survive as a testament to two remarkable individuals.

Martin Harrison

Elvis Presley

In October of 1944, when a riot of teenaged girls erupted during a Frank Sinatra appearance at the Paramount Theatre in New York, Elvis Aron Presley was still one year away from his first public performance for a children's radio talent contest in his hometown of Tupelo, Mississippi. As to the outcome of this competition there is some debate, but there can be no question that, by the evening of November 15, 1956, when the movie *Love Me Tender* opened at the same Paramount Theatre, decked out for the occasion with a thirty-foot-tall cardboard cutout of the now twenty-one-year-old star, Presley had pioneered a territory that Sinatra and his generation would never explore.

In 1956 Elvis was a rocket. Backed by Scotty Moore (guitar), Bill Black (stand-up bass), and D. J. Fontana (drums), he careened through more than fifty cities, moving beyond his southern base into the Midwest and the West Coast, and at each stop it was harder for the musicians to hear their instruments over the roar of the audience, until finally they were reduced to keeping time with Presley's bouncing behind. He made his first TV appearance in January and by September commanded the highest ratings ever (and the biggest fee) on the Ed Sullivan Show. He released his first LP in March and it became the first album to sell a million copies. November's movie star had his first screen test in April. A stunningly efficient publicity and marketing campaign orchestrated by his management fed him into the maw of a vast media machine oiled by an expanding consumer economy, and it in turn regurgitated millions of words and images that were mostly irrelevant to his true significance.

With what gifts did Presley conquer a nation? His musicianship and his way with a song. His melding of country and blues into rock and roll. His haunting voice, which he and his producers enhanced with glowing echoes in recordings. His intense sexual magnetism. His grasp of the dark poetry of everyday America. Obviously all of this, but also something else: an innate and uncalculating eye for the future of style in an increasingly visual culture that was fixated on the newest model. To be cool, he had to look cool, and to look cool, he had to shop creatively on the fringes of society. To buy his clothing in the stores along Memphis' Beale Street that catered mostly to a hip black clientele. To deepen the shadows around his eyes with makeup. To pick up moves at All-Night Gospel Singings. To study Marlon Brando and James Dean in darkened theaters. To paint a new Cadillac pink and give it to his mom.

In the spring of 1956, Elvis played Little Rock and Des Moines; Kansas City, Detroit, and Columbus; Oakland, LA, and Las Vegas; Savannah, Augusta, Charlotte, and Richmond; San Antonio and Corpus Christi and Waco and Amarillo, and numerous cities and towns in between. Marvin Israel, traveling with Edwin Miller, a writer for *Seventeen,* caught up with him in late May in Dayton, Ohio, hanging out with the band in the fieldhouse at the city's university before a pair of shows. Afterward, they all flew back to Memphis, where Elvis got some much needed R&R. For a brief moment on Presley's trip to the top, Israel was there, and photographed the essence of his cool.

Eric Himmel

The Show

Scotty Moore noticed in March that there was new electricity in the air when Elvis performed. Halls now had to hire extra security guards and police worked overtime when he was in town. Less than a week before the Dayton concerts seen here, a rampaging crowd in Kansas City had destroyed the band's drums and bass. Elvis was enjoying himself, experimenting with his mesmerizing powers. "I'll bet I could burp and make them squeal," he boasted to one of his recording-session backup singers. The engagements all had a common shape, and they weren't really over until the conquering hero had retired from the field of battle, at which point the announcement would come over the public address system, "Elvis has left the building." This was soon to become an all-purpose catchphrase for America's teenagers.

Love Me Tender

When *Love Me Tender* opened at New York City's Paramount Theatre at 8:00 in the morning of November 15, there were more than a thousand teenagers waiting on line to get in, with various fan clubs in attendance. It was a lot of kids for a Thursday when school was in session, and more than a few got sent packing by truant officers. Whether out of personal curiosity or because he was considering a follow-up piece for the magazine, Israel came down to Times Square to document the scene. Interviews with people leaving the early shows revealed a strong enthusiasm for the star but some disappointment that the movie was a conventional drama. They wanted rock & roll.

DAVID
WAYNE
"UPROARIOUS!"
GORDON HERLIE SMITH
THE MATCH MAKER
JUDY HOLLIDAY
Bells are Ringing
JULE STYNE
POLICE LINE
POLICE
DO NO
DEPT

Home

Dayton was Presley's last stop in a swing through the Midwest, and from there he returned home to Memphis with Israel and Miller in tow. Here, they found Presley's parents Gladys and Vernon in the new house their son had purchased for them. It had seven rooms, including a playroom and a den, where Israel photographed Elvis' high school diploma hanging on the wall. During this brief interlude when Presley was a superstar without a superstar's security apparatus, the house was not protected by a fence and was overrun with fans seeking autographs who were welcomed with good humor by the family. Presley, who explained ingenuously to a newspaper reporter later that year that "I've made a study of Marlon Brando," spent his brief holiday from touring buzzing around town on his new Harley-Davidson motorcycle with his local girlfriend. He treated her to a hat like his.

Memphis City Schools

DIPLOMA

This Certifies That _____ Elvis Aron Presley _____ having completed the Course of Study prescribed by the Board of Education of the Memphis City Schools in the

L. C. HUMES HIGH SCHOOL

of this City, and having sustained a correct moral deportment, is entitled to this

TESTIMONIAL

the highest honor in our power to bestow and is leaving the school with the respect and confidence of the Board and Instructors, and with their best wishes for continued success. In Testimony Whereof, the President and Secretary of the Board of Education, the Superintendent of Schools, and the Principal have affixed their signatures at Memphis, Tennessee the 2nd day of June 1953.

Milton Bowers
President

O. H. Jones
Secretary

Ernest C. Ball
Superintendent

T. C. Brindley
Principal

Author's Acknowledgments

I should especially like to thank Lawrence Israel, the artist's cousin, whose company, cooperation, and generosity throughout have made this project a pleasure. My grateful thanks also to Richard Eagan, who first asked me to write about Marvin, Shelley Dowell, whose help and enthusiasm have been invaluable, and Eric Himmel, both as friend and editor. My most sincere thanks are no less due to Jacqueline Ayer, Lillian Bassman, Terry Boxall, Ann Giordano, Amanda Harrison, Ben Harrison, and Paul Himmel.

This book is dedicated to the memory of Sally Israel.

Library of Congress Cataloging-in-Publication Data
Israel, Marvin.
    Elvis Presley 1956 / photographs by Marvin Israel ;
    edited and designed by Martin Harrison.
        p.   cm.
    ISBN 0–8109–0899–9
    1. Presley, Elvis, 1935–1977—Portraits.
    2. Rock musicians—United States—Portraits.
    I. Harrison, Martin, 1945– .
  II. Title.
ML88.P76I87 1998
782.42166'092—dc21   98–19606

Printed and bound in Italy

Harry N. Abrams, Inc.
100 Fifth Avenue
New York, N.Y. 10011
www.abramsbooks.com